The Power of the

DELTICS

Frontispiece **55 021** *Argyll & Sutherland Highlander* is framed between upper quadrants at Black Carr Junction, south of Doncaster, as it heads the Sunday 10.00 Kings Cross-Aberdeen on 6 February 1977.

G. W. Morrison

The Power of the

DELTICS

by J.S. Whiteley &
G.W. Morrison

Acknowledgement

The authors would like to thank all the photographers who
have so kindly contributed pictures, G.E.C. Traction Ltd for
their assistance in making early material available and The
Public Relations Department at British Rail, York, for
granting facilities which made many of these photographs
possible.

First published 1977
Reprinted 1986
This impression 2004

ISBN 0 902888 97 8

Published by Oxford Publishing Co.

an imprint of Ian Allan Publishing Ltd, Hersham, Surrey KT12 4RG.
Printed by Ian Allan Printing Ltd, Hersham, Surrey KT12 4RG.

Code: 0407/A

Publisher's note: This book is reprinted, as a tribute to the 'Deltics', as originally
published in 1977. The reader will appreciate that over the last 27 years there have
been many changes, with *Deltic* and six production examples surviving in
preservation.

Introduction

This book is an attempt to portray a record of the Deltic locomotives from the appearance of the prototype Deltic in 1955, to their workings in 1976. We have deliberately not included too many technical details about the locomotives, nor the reasons why it was necessary for the East Coast main line to have replacements for an ageing fleet of steam locomotives and underpowered main line diesels, as these subject have been discussed in great detail by the railway press during the last 15 years. Suffice it to say the introduction of the Deltics to the East Coast main line services was a brilliant piece of detailed planning and forward thinking, as these locomotives were still performing the very exacting duties set them, 16 years after introduction of the production models.

Before orders were placed with English Electric by the British Transport Commission, extensive trials were conducted with the prototype Deltic over the West Coast and East Coast main lines during a period of almost 2¹/₂ years, and in the Spring of 1958 the British Railways Board ordered 22 locomotives to be delivered commencing 1960. This contract included an important penalty clause, whereby, if the locomotives did not achieve their scheduled mileage, the British Transport Commission would reduce the sum paid to English Electric for maintenance and engine overhauls. Delays occurred during construction and D9001, which was the first locomotive to be completed, did not arrive at Finsbury Park until March 1961.

The prototype soldiered on until 1961 when it returned to the English Electric Vulcan Works having covered 400,000 miles. In spite of this colossal mileage, certain aspects of the Deltic engines were not considered absolutely reliable, and it took a considerable time with very concentrated supervision and thorough maintenance by English Electric staff before the production locomotives were achieving about 180,000 miles or more per annum. Subsequently the prototype was presented to the Science Museum by English Electric and can now be seen on display at the National Railway Museum, York.

There was much speculation about the design and livery of the production models prior to their appearance although it was known that the rather flamboyant light blue, grey and cream livery of the prototype would not be adopted. In the event they appeared in a somewhat conservative but pleasing two-tone green livery, with rather more rounded ends to improve visibility from the cab. This livery was retained basically for about eight years before British Rail adopted the now standard blue livery, which when applied to these prestige locomotives rendered their appearance very dull and unimaginative in the opinion of the authors.

The story of the Baby Deltics, as they became known, is less successful. These 10 locomotives were produced in 1959 and were powered by a single 1,100hp nine-cylinder Deltic engine, but after about three years; service on secondary passenger duties on the Eastern Region, all but one had been taken out of service and banished to Stratford for store. In 1965 they re-appeared in traffic after modifications, and gave reliable service for a few years on London suburban services, before being withdrawn from 1968 because of their non-standard design.

The second Deltic prototype, DP2, carried out extensive running on the Eastern Region main line and was subject to intensive working for technical and development reasons. At one stage it covered the incredible distance of 43,000 miles in eight weeks which is understood to be a record for any locomotive in this country. This locomotive came to a premature end near Thirsk, in a collision which is illustrated in this book.

In 1976 the Deltics were still intensively rostered for handling the principle East Coast Inter City services, but with the introduction of the HSTs in 1978 were then relegated to secondary main line duties.

J. S. Whiteley
G. W. Morrison

1 *(above)* The prototype Deltic during construction at Dick, Kerr Works, Preston in 1955. Other locomotives which can be seen in the foreground from left to right include 1500 hp, 2Co-Co2 diesel electric for New Zealand, 750 hp. Bo-Bo diesel electric for Nigeria and 0-6-0 diesel electric 350 hp. shunting locomotive for the Netherlands.

2 *(left)* The prototype emerging from Dick, Kerr Works on accommodation bogies late in 1955...

3 *(below)* ... and seen outside the works before entering service. *All photographs GEC Traction Ltd*

4 *(above)* The prototype Deltic underwent trials on the
Settle-Carlisle line and is seen here near Armathwaite with
a dynamometer car.   *GEC Traction Ltd.*

5 *(below)* On 13 September 1960 the prototype is seen at
Oakleigh Park on a Hull-Kings Cross train.

                                                    D. Cross.

6 *(above)* Here, the prototype Deltic speeds through Stafford on 11 August 1958 heading the up "Manxman".
B. Morrison

7 *(below)* The prototype is seen in the bay at Doncaster before working an up express.
British Rail

8 *(above)* The ten class 23 Bo-Bo diesel electrics were powered by a small 9 cylinder Napier "Deltic" engine of 1100 hp. and became known as "Baby Deltics". Newly completed D5902 is seen outside the paint shop at Doncaster on Sunday 3 May 1959.

G. W. Morrison

9 *(below)* The first in the class, No. D5900 leaving Kings Cross on 10 August 1960.　　*J. K. Morton*

10 (*above*) No. D5903 near Hadley Wood, in July 1959 heading a Kings Cross-Welwyn local.

11 (*right*) D5909 emerges from Welwyn tunnel in October 1960 with a Cambridge-Kings Cross train.

12 (*below*) No. D5902 near Brookmans Park on an up Suburban train in July 1960.

All photographs D. Cross

13 *(above)* Baby Deltic No. D5908 approaches Oakleigh Park on a down Suburban train in July 1960.

D. Cross

14 *(right)* The end of the line for D5901 seen at Doncaster on 3 October 1976 after removal from the Research Centre at Derby.

G. W. Morrison

15 (*above*) DP2 was a Co-Co development of the English Electric Class 40 but externally looked very much like a Deltic. It is seen leaving Leeds Central on 18 February 1967 heading the Bradford portion of the "White Rose Pullman".

G. W. Morrison

16 (*below*) Nunnery Junction, Sheffield sees DP2 passing on 5 October 1965 with the 11.20 Kings Cross-Sheffield (Midland) which includes Pullman coaches.

L. A. Nixon

17 *(above)* DP2 at Leeds Central on the down "White Rose Pullman".　*G. W. Morrison*

18 *(above left)* It is seen waiting to leave Sheffield Midland on the 15.15 to Kings Cross.　*L. A. Nixon*

19 *(above right)* . . . and waiting to leave Bradford Exchange on the "White Rose Pullman". 18 February 1967.　*G. W. Morrison*

20 *(right)* DP2 emerges from the tunnel between Stanningley and Laisterdyke on the Bradford portion of the "White Rose Pullman".　*L. A. Nixon*

21 *(above)* On 24 July 1962 DP2 enters Crewe from the North.   *N. Stead*

22 & 23 The end came for DP2 in an unfortuna[te] manner whilst working t[he] 12.00 Kings Cross-Edinburgh express. The accident occurred near Thirsk due to it collidin[g] at speed with a derailed cement train on the dow[n] slow line. 31 July 1967.
Photos J. M. Boy[d]

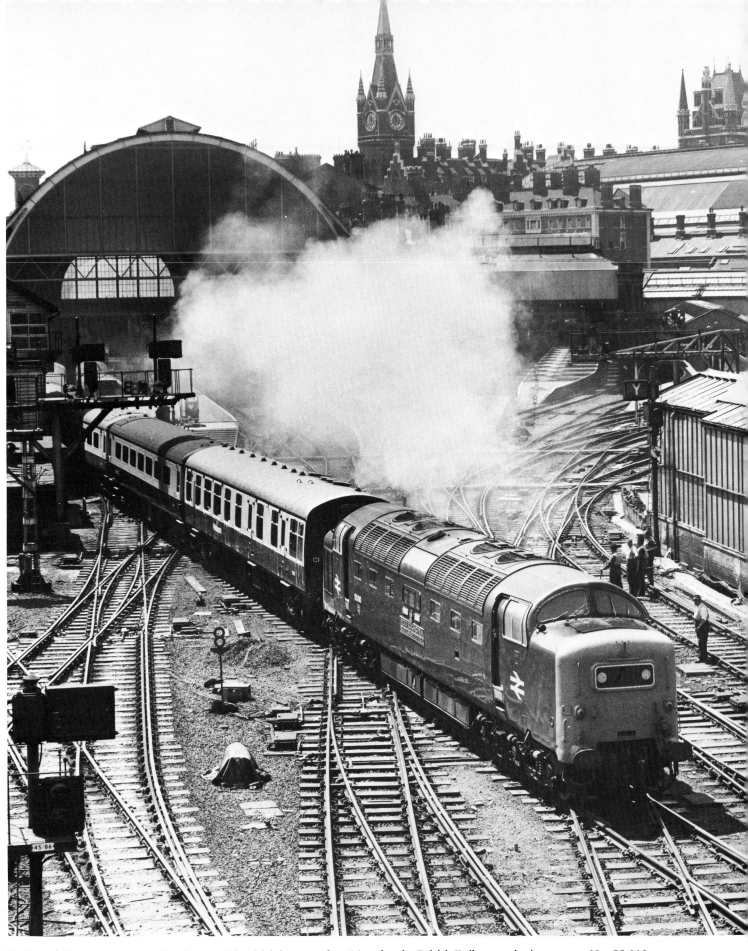

24 One of the twenty-two production models which became class 55 under the British Rail re-numbering system. No. 55 010
The King's Own Scottish Borderer leaves Kings Cross on 19 June 1975 heading the 11.45 to Newcastle. This was the first
Deltic to achieve 2 million miles.   *B. Morrison*

Transition at Leeds.
25 *(left)* Leeds City on Sunday 21 October 1962.
J. S. Whiteley

26 *(middle left)* Leeds Central on 7 September 1963.
J. M. Rayner

27 *(middle right)* The "Queen of Scots" with D9016 alongside the up "White Rose" at Leeds Central.
G. W. Morrison

28 *(bottom)* Evening rush hour at Leeds Central on 18 April 1964.
J. S. Whiteley

29 *(above)* D9008 as yet unnamed, passing Holbeck High
Level on the 17.29 Leeds Central-Kings Cross. 5 June 1962.
G. W. Morrison

30 *(below)* In contrast 55 015 *Tulyar* ready to leave the
new Leeds City on the 11.30 to Kings Cross. 4 May 1976.
G. W. Morrison

Above With the skyline of Newcastle visible on the horizon, 55 017 *The Durham Light Infantry* accelerates the 08.00 Edinburgh-Kings Cross past Bensham. 7 August 1976.

P. J. Robinson

Left D9018 *Ballymoss* is seen in its original two-tone green livery before the addition of the yellow nose panel, heading the up "Flying Scotsman" near Little Ponton on 7 July 1962.

G. W. Morrison

Above 55 007 *Pinza* heading the Sunday 12.00 Kings Cross-Edinburgh on the very picturesque stretch of the East Coast main line near Burnmouth on 20 July 1975.

Mrs D. A. Robinson

Below 55 013 *The Black Watch*, just ex-works, approaches York on a running-in turn, returning to Doncaster on 11 December 1976.

J. S. Whiteley

31 (*above*) D9000 in original two-tone green livery brings the empty stock of the up "Talisman" through Princes Street Gardens, Edinburgh on 17 July 1961. *J. S. Whiteley*

32 (*below*) With the clock of the North British Hotel showing five minutes past ten No. D9019 *Royal Highland Fusilier* leaves Edinburgh Waverley on the up "Flying Scotsman". 30 May 1966. *J. S. Whiteley*

33 *(above)* Durham Cathedral dominates this picture of 55 022 *Royal Scots Grey* on the 14.00 Kings Cross-Edinburgh. 26 May 1974.   *I. S. Carr*

34 *(below)* No. 9001 *St. Paddy* crossing the Wearmouth Bridge at Sunderland on the 13.30 Newcastle-Kings Cross via the coast route. 15 April 1973.   *I. S. Carr*

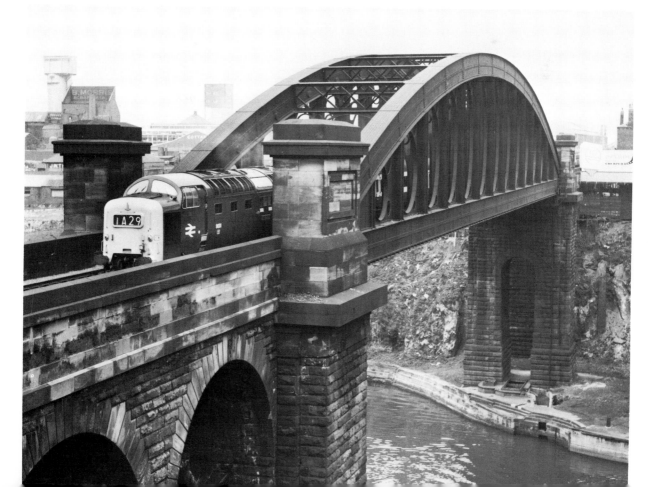

Above 55 021 *Argyll & Sutherland Highlander* at Croxdale, between Durham and Ferryhill, on the up "Flying Scotsman". 20 September 1975.

Mrs D. A. Robinson

Left Nameplate of 55 021.   G. W. Morrison

Below D9020 *Nimbus* in two-tone green but with yellow nose panel approaches Alnmouth on a Kings Cross-Edinburgh express. 21 May 1966.

G. W. Morrison

ARGYLL & SUTHERLAND HIGHLANDER

Above 55 012 *Crepello* near Beeston, Leeds, on the 17.30 to Kings Cross. 25 June 1975.
G. W. Morrison

Right 55 012 *Crepello* passes the site of South Otterington station on the down "Talisman". 26 August 1975.
G. W. Morrison

Below 55 015 *Tulyar* leaving York on the S.O. 10.48 Newcastle-Kings Cross. 11 December 1976.

J. S. Whiteley

The 11.55 Bradford Exchange — Kings Cross

35 *(above)* No. 55 022 *Royal Scots Grey* climbing the 1 in 50 near Hammerton Street diesel depot on 7 July 1976. *G. W. Morrison*

36 *(above right)* 55 003 *Meld* rounding the sharp curve on the 1 in 50 at St. Dunstans. 23 March 1976. *J. S. Whiteley*

37 *(below right)* 55 012 *Crepello* passing the site of Laisterdyke station on 30 June 1976. *G. W. Morrison*

Left Today's standardised blue livery with that powerful nose exaggerated by the yellow high visibility paintwork seems very unimaginative by comparison with the original livery as seen in the picture in the centre of the opposite page. 55 015 *Tulyar* is seen running light engine through Princes Street Gardens, Edinburgh, prior to working the up "Flying Scotsman" on 7 June 1975.

G. W. Morrison

Below 55 008 *The Green Howards* leaves Kings Cross on the 17.00 to Edinburgh on 10 July 1976.

G. W. Morrison

Above 55 008 *The Green Howards* is seen again, this time at Beningbrough on the 14.00 Kings Cross-Edinburgh. 15 September 1975.

G. W. Morrison

Right D9001 *St. Paddy* passes Wakefield MPD on the 14.05 Leeds-Doncaster stopper when this train was being used for crew training. 7 September 1961.

G. W. Morrison

Below 55 004 *Queen's Own Highlander* glitters in the evening sunshine as it leaves Ardsley tunnel on the 17.30 Leeds-Kings Cross. 23 September 1975.

G. W. Morrison

38 *(above)* A bird's eye view of the east end of Newcastle Central. D9006 *The Fife & Forfar Yeomanry* leaves on the 08.00 Kings Cross-Edinburgh.

J. M. Boyes

39 *(right)* 9000 *Royal Scots Grey* on the left leaving Newcastle in pouring rain on the 17.00 to Kings Cross alongside 9011 *The Royal Northumberland Fusiliers* standing on the 17.23 to York. 6 July 1973. *I. S. Carr*

40 *(above)* A humble duty for D9002 *The King's Own York-shire Light Infantry* seen near Durham on a down freight on 1 June 1963.   *I. S. Carr*

41 *(below)* . . . and seen again as 55 002 crossing Chester-le Street viaduct on an up Newcastle-Kings Cross. 1 April 1975.   *I. S. Carr*

Above D9013 *The Black Watch* leaves Bradford Exchange on the up "White Rose Pullman". 11 July 1966.

G. W. Morrison

Bottom 55 001 *St. Paddy* heads north after its Peterborough stop on the 14.00 Kings Cross-Aberdeen. 16 October 1976.

J. S. Whiteley

Right A broadside view showing the full 69′ 6″ of 55 020 *Nimbus* backing into Kings Cross to work a down express. 10 July 1976.

G. W. Morrison

Centre 55 015 *Tulyar* comes off the King Edward Bridge at Gateshead on the 08.00 Edinburgh-Kings Cross. 3 July 1976.

P. A. Robinson

Bottom An unidentified Deltic races southwards near Beningbrough against a setting sun over the Vale of York. 15 September 1975.

G. W. Morrison

42 (above) D9021, the last Deltic to enter service, passes Copley Hill MPD, Leeds, on the down "West Riding". 4 October 1962.   G. W. Morrison

43 (right) D9001 *St. Paddy* leaving Leeds Central on the up "Harrogate Sunday Pullman". 1 July 1962.
       J. S. Whiteley

44 (below) D9020 *Nimbus* passing Beeston Junction on the 17.29 Leeds Central-Kings Cross. 7 June 1962.
       G. W. Morrison

45 (above) 55 017 *The Durham Light Infantry* passing Lofthouse Colliery, near Wakefield, on the 17.30 Inter-City from Leeds to Kings Cross. 27 July 1976.   *G. W. Morrison*

46 (below) D9010 takes the Harrogate line at Wortley Junction, Leeds, on the down "Queen of Scots Pullman". 28 May 1963.   *J. S. Whiteley*

47 *(above)* D9017 passing Stoke summit on a down express. 21 July 1962.   *G. W. Morrison*

48 *(below)* D9007 *Pinza* emerges from Stoke tunnel on an up express on 7 July 1962.   *G. W. Morrison*

49 *(above)* 55 017 *The Durham Light Infantry* leaving Stoke tunnel and passing the now disused High Dyke sidings on a northbound Inter-City express. 23 February 1974.

T. Boustead

50 *(below)* D9019 on the up "Flying Scotsman" leaving Stoke tunnel on 21 July 1962. *G. W. Morrison*

51 (*above*) The magnificent arched roof of York covers D9003 *Meld* as it leaves platform 9 on 2 May 1964 for Newcastle.   *J. S. Whiteley*

52 (*below*) 55 014 *The Duke of Wellington's Regiment* curves northwards from York on the Sunday 12.00 Kings Cross-Edinburgh. 19 September 1976.

J. S. Whiteley

53 *(above)* The Sunday 10.00 Edinburgh Waverley-Kings Cross passes under Holgate Bridge, York behind 55 003 *Meld*. 19 September 1976. *J. S. Whiteley*

54 *(below)* . . . and seen from the same bridge behind 55 015 *Tulyar* on 10 October 1976. *J. S. Whiteley*

Southbound from Doncaster

55 (*above*) D9002 leaving on an up Leeds train.
17 June 1962. *G. W. Morrison*

56 (*left*) D9004 passing through the centre road
on the up "Flying Scotsman" displaying the
short-lived thistle emblem. 4 April 1964.
J. S. Whiteley

57 (*below*) Dominated by the "Plant" and with
a steam standby on the right, D9019 leaves for
Kings Cross on 29 April 1962. *G. W. Morrison*

Northbound from Doncaster

58 *(above)* 55 015 *Tulyar* leaving on the 12.10 Kings Cross-
Aberdeen. 24 February 1976.   *J. S. Whiteley*

59 *(below)* D9016 passes under the Great North Road on
a down express. 14 May 1963.   *J. S. Whiteley*

60 (*above*) Clearly displaying the "Flying Scotsman" headboard, D9007 *Pinza* passes through Selby on 13 December 1962.   *J. S. Whiteley*

61 (*below*) 55 015 *Tulyar* crossing the famous swing bridge at Selby on the up "Flying Scotsman". 20 March 1976.   *J. S. Whiteley*

62 *(above)* The down "Talisman" is accelerated away from Selby by 55 022 *Royal Scots Grey* with Drax Power Station visible on the horizon. 10 May 1976.

G. W. Morrison

63 *(below)* 55 008 *The Green Howards* accelerates the 09.00 Kings Cross-Newcastle past Barlby, just north of Selby on 20 November 1976.

N. Stead

64 (*above*) Skirting the coast line north of Berwick, 55 017 *The Durham Light Infantry* is about to cross the border from Scotland to England on the 16.00 Edinburgh-Kings Cross in June 1976.   *L. A. Nixon*

65 (*below*) A panoramic view of Edinburgh Waverley taken from above Calton tunnel; an unidentified Deltic leaves the east end of the station on the up "Flying Scotsman". 23 July 1963.   *J. S. Whiteley*

66 *(above)* Displaying the ornate thistle emblem carried by the "Flying Scotsman", D9019 prepares to leave Edinburgh Waverley on 30 May 1966.   *J. S. Whiteley*

67 *(below)* D9007 *Pinza* passes Innerwick signal box at the start of the climb to Grantshouse on the up "Queen of Scots Pullman" in 1968.   *D. Cross*

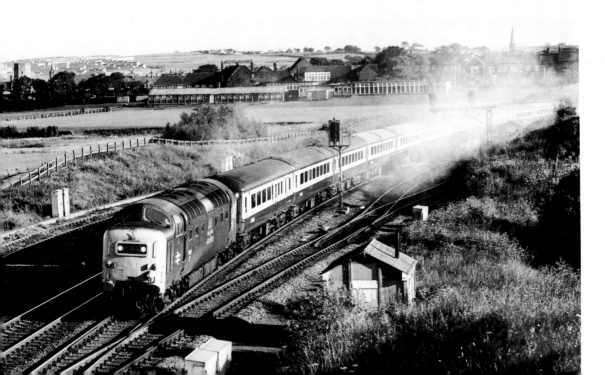

68 *(above)* The 08.00 Kings
Cross -Edinburgh behind
55 013 *The Black Watch*
glitters in wintry sunshine
on the Royal Border
Bridge as it approaches
Berwick-upon-Tweed
station. 14 December 197
B. Morriso

69 *(left)* 55 022 *Royal
Scots Grey* leaving
Berwick-upon-Tweed on
the 14.00 ex Kings Cross.
28 June 1976.
G. W. Morriso

70 *(above)* 55 009 *Alycidon* passing High Dyke signal box on the 12.00 Kings Cross-Aberdeen. 23 February 1974.

T. Boustead

71 *(left)* Nameplate of 55 009.

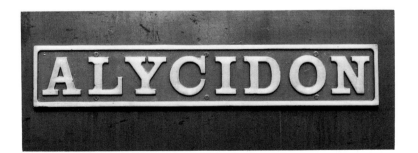

ALYCIDON

72 The Castle Keep affords a splendid view of the east end of Newcastle and in this picture *55 019 Royal Highland Fusilier* is seen leaving for Edinburgh on the 07.45 ex Kings Cross on 3 November 1976.

J. S. Whiteley

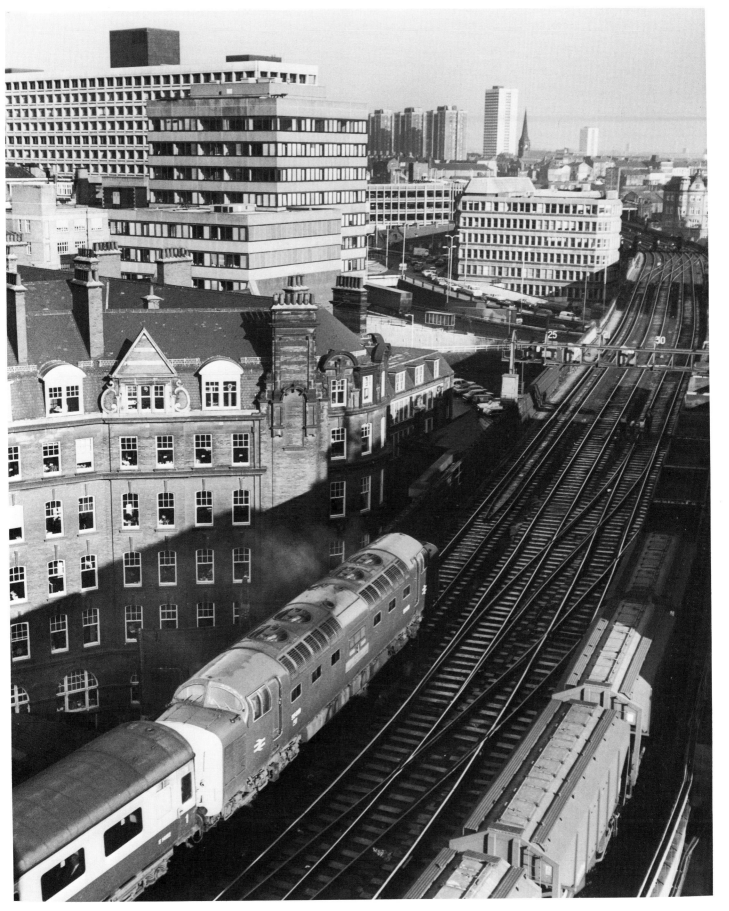

73 . . . and gathers speed past a blend of old and new architecture on its way out of Newcastle.   *J. S. Whiteley*

74 *(above)* D9003 *Meld* off the rails outside Leeds City.
J. S. Whiteley

75 *(above)* . . . and on the rails inside Leeds Central.
G. W. Morrison

76 *(above)* D9019 nears Beeston Junction, Leeds, on the down "West Riding". 25 April 1962. *G. W. Morrison*

77 *(below)* D9021 *Argyll & Sutherland Highlander* at Wortley South, Leeds, on an up express. 28 April 1967.
G. W. Morrison

Pullmans at Leeds

78 *(above)* D9016 at Leeds Central on 2 October 1962 on the down "Queen of Scots Pullman".

G. W. Morrison

79 *(left)* D9008 *The Green Howards* rounds the curve at Wortley South Junction, Leeds, on the up "Queen of Scots Pullman". *L. A. Nixon*

80 *(below)* D9013 *The Black Watch* leaving Leeds Central on the up "Queen of Scots Pullman" on 18 April 1964. *J. S. Whiteley*

81 *(above)* Against a background of castle and cathedral, 55 017 *The Durham Light Infantry* climbs away from Durham with the 15.10 Newcastle-Kings Cross on 27 May 1974.

I. S. Carr

82 *(below)* D9012 *Crepello* on the up "Flying Scotsman" in wintry conditions at Durham on 28 December 1962.

I. S. Carr

83 (left) The Billingham Beck branch single line tablet is handed over by the Haverton Hill South box signalman to the crew of D9014 *The Duke of Wellington's Regiment* on the diverted 13.30 Newcastle-Sunderland-Kings Cross on Sunday 13 June 1965.

I. S. Carr

84 (below) Watering a Deltic the hard way (from too short a water column bag) at Stockton on 29 April 1962. D9017 had been diverted via Brompton and Sedgefield on the Sunday 10.00 Kings Cross-Edinburgh.

I. S. Carr

Southern departures from York

85 (*above*) 55 014 *The Duke of Wellington's Regiment* nears
Chaloners Whin Junction on the 11.40 Edinburgh-Kings
Cross. 20 March 1976.   *J. S. Whiteley*

86 (*below*) 55 006 *The Fife & Forfar Yeomanry* passes
Dringhouses on the Sunday 10.00 Edinburgh-Kings Cross
on 24 October 1976.   *J. S. Whiteley*

Northern departures from York

87 *(above)* 55 011 *The Royal Northumberland Fusiliers* passes York Yard North at Clifton, heading the Sunday 10.00 Kings Cross-Aberdeen on 24 October 1976.

J. S. Whiteley

88 *(below)* D9021 leaving platform 9 on 19 October 1963.

J. S. Whiteley

89 (above) 55 017 *The Durham Light Infantry* accelerating a southbound express past Bridge Junction, Doncaster on 14 August 1975.

L. A. Nixon

90 (below) With Doncaster MPD in the background 55 001 *St. Paddy* approaches Bridge Junction from the South.

J. M. Rayner

91 *(above)* On 5 February 1977 55 002 *The King's Own Yorkshire Light Infantry* heading mark II air-conditioned stock leaving Doncaster with the 11.25 Kings Cross-Harrogate.
J. S. Whiteley

92 *(below)* . . . and in contrast D9016 in two-tone green livery on maroon coaches leaving on the down "White Rose" on 14 May 1963.
J. S. Whiteley

93, 94, 96, 96 Deltics on Haymarket shed, April 1976.

G. W. Morrison

97 (above) D9018 *Ballymoss* crossing the Royal Border Bridge in June 1972 on a down express.   *D. Cross*

98 (below) . . . and 55 011 *Royal Northumberland Fusiliers* in wintry sunshine heads South with the 08.55 Aberdeen-Kings Cross. 14 December 1974.   *B. Morrison*

99, 100 55 001 *St. Paddy* calls at Peterborough on the 14.00 Kings Cross-Aberdeen on 16 October 1976.

Above J. S. Whiteley, below G. W. Morrison

101, 102 . . . this sequence of four pictures clearly shows the rebuilt layout. *Above J. S. Whiteley, below G. W. Morrison*

103 *(above)* Under the shadow of York Minster 55 019 *Royal Highland Fusilier* passes a line-up of diesels outside the motive power depot on the Sunday 11.00 Edinburgh-Kings Cross. *J. S. Whiteley*

104 *(below)* . . . and after a brief stop at York accelerating away from Chaloners Whin Junction on its way South. Note the latest modifications to the route indicator panel which British Rail no longer use. *J. S. Whiteley*

105 (right) 55 016 *Gordon Highlander* leaves York for the north on the "Aberdonian". *J. S. Whiteley*

106 (below) ... and meets 55 001 *St. Paddy* arriving on the 11.25 Edinburgh-Kings Cross on 9 October 1976. *J. S. Whiteley*

107 *(above)* A group of five class 47s surround 55 005 *The Prince of Wales's Own Regiment of Yorkshire* in Kings Cross yard on 10 July 1976.

G. W. Morrison

108 *(left)* Super power in Kings Cross yard in the form of Deltics 55 012, 55 021 and 55 003 awaiting their next turns of duty to the north. 7 March 1976.

G. W. Morrison

109 *(above right)* The 16.00 to Edinburgh leaves Kings Cross behind 55 018 *Ballymoss* whilst 55 015 *Tulyar* heads for the yard for servicing. 10 July 1976.

G. W. Morrison

110 *(below right)* 55 006 *The Fife & Forfar Yeomanry* enters Gas Works Tunnel, Kings Cross on the 12.00 to Aberdeen. 10 July 1976. *G. W. Morrison*

111 *(above)* **55 001** *St. Paddy* awaiting departure from Kings Cross with the 22.15 "Night Aberdonian" on 6 December 1974. *B. Morrison*

112 (right) 55 001 *St. Paddy* takes a rest inside Kings Cross after arrival on an overnight sleeper. 25 September 1976.

G. W. Morrison

113 (below) 55 018 *Ballymoss* threads its way out of Kings Cross with the 11.25 Inter-City to Leeds. 12 June 1975.   B. Morrison

114, 115, 116 At 09.59 the last passengers are boarding the "Flying Scotsman" at Kings Cross, the second man looks at his watch in the cab of 55 011 and at 10.01 *The Royal Northumberland Fusiliers* departs.

All photographs G. W. Morrison

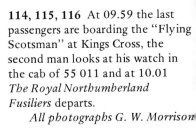

17 (above) The "Night
Aberdonian" ready to
leave Kings Cross
behind 9001 St. Paddy.
November 1973.
B. Morrison

18 (right) A powerful
picture of an immacu-
late Deltic in original
livery about to leave
Kings Cross on the
down "Flying Scots-
man".

National Railway
Museum Collection

119, 120, 121 Kings Cross yard on 7 March 1976 and
10 July 1971.   *G. W. Morrison above, N. E. Preedy below.*

(right) 9012 *Crepello* ⟨emer⟩ges from Copenhagen ⟨Tun⟩nel at Belle Isle with an ⟨up e⟩xpress on 22 March 1973.

B. Morrison

(below) 9017 *The ⟨Dur⟩ham Light Infantry* ⟨eme⟩rges from the other end ⟨of C⟩openhagen Tunnel into ⟨even⟩ing sunshine as it heads ⟨nort⟩h with the "Talisman". ⟨18 S⟩eptember 1973.

B. Morrison

124 *(above)* 55 012 *Crepello* eases the 17.40 Bradford-Leeds-Kings Cross round the sharp curve at Gelderd Road, Leeds. 14 July 1976.   *G. W. Morrison*

125 *(below)* 55 022 *Royal Scots Grey* gets into its stride at Beeston, Leeds on the 17.30 Leeds-Kings Cross. 14 June 1976.   *G. W. Morrison*

126, 127 Two pictures of the down "Leeds Executive" Inter-City express headed on both occasions by 55 012 *Crepello* seen above passing the site of Beeston station, Leeds on 14 June 1976 and below approaching what was formerly Beeston Junction on 28 June 1976. *G. W. Morrison*

128 The "Flying Scotsman" departs from Kings Cross behind 55 017 *The Durham Light Infantry* on 12 June 1975.

B. Morrison

129, 130 On the last day of the Railway Correspondence and Travel Society ran a special train from Leeds to Edinburgh and return hauled by D9007 *Pinza* seen above at Riccarton Junction and below at Fountainhall during photographic stops.
5 January 1969.

G. W. Morrison

131 (above) D9005 *The Prince of Wales's Own Regiment of Yorkshire* races through Kirkstall on the outskirts of Leeds on the return "Hadrian Flyer" on 17 June 1967. This locomotive covered the 86.8 miles from Carlisle to Skipton over Ais Gill in what is believed to be a record time of 72 minutes 47 seconds.

G. W. Morrison

132 (below) 55 003 *Meld* heads a special from Paddington to Cardiff past Ebbw Junction depot, Newport on 12 October 1975.

B. J. Nicolle

Deltics on the West Coast
133, 134, 135 Due to bridge
repairs at Dunbar on 23 July 1972
East Coast trains were diverted from
Edinburgh via Carstairs and Carlisle
to Newcastle. 1E17 headed by
D9019 is seen passing Beattock
Summit, 1E09 with D9002 at
Strawfrank Junction, Carstairs
and 1E13 passing Wandel Mill,
Lamington behind D9006.

Photographs D. Cross

Deltic Wanderings

136 (*above*) D9007 *Pinza* leaving Riccarton Junction on R.C.T.S. special from Leeds to Edinburgh on 5 January 1969.   *N. Stead*

137 (*right*) Before its naming ceremony at Inverness, D9019 *Royal Highland Fusilier* is seen at Aviemore piloting D5338 on the morning mail from Perth to Inverness. 15 April 1969.   *D. Cross*

138 (*below*) The 10.10 Kings Cross-Leeds approaches Leeds from the east as it curves off the branch from Castleford at Garforth.   *J. M. Rayner*

139 *(above)* 55 001 *St. Paddy* negotiates the sharp curve off the line from Hitchin at Shepreth Branch Junction, just south of Cambridge and joins the Great Eastern Line with the Sunday 13.00 Kings Cross-Edinburgh, diverted via Cambridge due to engineering work on the main line near Sandy. 7 November 1976.   *G. W. Morrison*

140 *(below)* On the same date 55 017 *The Durham Light Infantry* restarts the 14.00 Kings Cross-Edinburgh at Cambridge North after pausing to pick up a pilotman.
        G. W. Morrison

141 *(above)* The up "Flying Scotsman" approaches Peterborough at speed behind 55 022 *Royal Scots Grey.*
16 October 1976.   *G. W. Morrison*

142 *(below)* 55 008 *The Green Howards* slows for its Doncaster stop on the Sunday 10.00 Kings Cross-Aberdeen on 7 November 1976.   *J. S. Whiteley*

143 *(above)* 55 015 *Tulyar* gets an enthusiastic wave at Berwick-upon-Tweed on a southbound express.

J. M. Rayner

144 *(below)* Silhouetted against the horizon, a Deltic crosses the high embankment between Tweedmouth and Berwick on a down Edinburgh express. 1 June 1976.

L. A. Nixon

145 *(above)* Running 18 minutes late due to fog, 55 015 *Tulyar* leaves Darlington on the 08.00 Kings Cross-Edinburgh on 22 October 1976.   *J. S. Whiteley*

146 *(below)* 55 009 *Alycidon* speeds towards Darlington near Croft on the down "Flying Scotsman". 22 October 1976.   *J. S. Whiteley*

147 *(above)* In the Newcastle suburbs at Manors, 55 016 *Gordon Highlander* accelerates the 08.00 Kings Cross-Edinburgh towards Heaton. 13 October 1976.

N. Stead

148 *(below)* 55 022 *Royal Scots Grey* rounds the curve off the King Edward Bridge at Gateshead on the up "Flying Scotsman". 3 November 1976. *J. S. Whiteley*

149 (above) The 07.45 Kings Cross-Edinburgh crosses Byker Bridge, Newcastle behind 55 019 *Royal Highland Fusilier*. 13 October 1976. *N. Stead*

150 (below) 55 009 *Alycidon* heads the 08.50 Aberdeen-Kings Cross at Benton Quarry, near Newcastle. 13 October 1976. *N. Stead*

151 (above) 55 020 *Nimbus* curves sharply away from the former Lancashire and Yorkshire line at St. Dunstans on the 11.55 Bradford-Kings Cross. 19 July 1976.

G. W. Morrison

152 (above right) 55 019 *Royal Highland Fusilier* leaves Bradford Exchange on 4 November 1975 with the 11.55 to Kings Cross.

G. W. Morrison

153 (below right) . . . and seen again at Laisterdyke.

G. W. Morrison

154 (*above*) The 17.30 Kings Cross-Leeds and Bradford emerges from Copenhagen Tunnel behind 9007 *Pinza* whilst 5800 moves a workmen's electrification train over the flyover towards Kings Cross Yards. 11 September 1973.

B. Morrison

155 (*below*) The 14.00 Kings Cross-Edinburgh heads northwards across Welwyn viaduct behind an unidentified Deltic on 6 November 1976.

G. W. Morrison

156 *(right)* D9003 *Meld* leaves Stockton with the 09.30 Glasgow (Queen Street)-Kings Cross diverted via Sedgefield and Yarm. 1 April 1962.   *I. S. Carr*

157 *(below)* D9008 *The Green Howards* on the down "Flying Scotsman" passes Hett Mill level crossing near Durham. 9 March 1969.   *J. M. Boyes*

158 *(above)* At Bishopton Lane Junction, Stockton-on-Tees D9020 *Nimbus* is seen avoiding the station on the 13.30 Newcastle-Kings Cross. 3 November 1968.

J. M. Boyes

159 *(below)* The down "Flying Scotsman" hurries past Darlington station headed by 55 018 *Ballymoss*. 23 May 1975.

I. S. Carr

160 (*right*) 9003 *Meld* passes Penshaw North with the 10.35 Newcastle-Kings Cross, diverted via Leamside. 2 September 1973. *I. S. Carr*

161 (*below*) Due to an accident at Ferryhill D9001 *St. Paddy* is seen approaching Relly Mill from the Bishop Auckland direction with the 11.00 Kings Cross-Glasgow. 24 July 1963. *I. S. Carr*

162 *(above)* The down "Flying Scotsman" passes non-stop through York behind D9012 *Crepello* on 19 October 1963.   *J. S. Whiteley*

163 *(below)* 55 014 *The Duke of Wellington's Regiment* leans to the curve at Clifton as it slows for York on the Sunday 11.00 Edinburgh-Kings Cross. 24 October 1976.   *G. W. Morrison*

164 (right) 9010 awaits departure from Kings Cross on the 20.30 to Edinburgh in November 1973.

N. E. Preedy

165 (below) Overnight mail from the north pauses at York.

J. M. Rayner

166 *(above)* The 15.00 Kings Cross-Newcastle approaches Riccall, north of Selby, behind 55 007 *Pinza*. 18 August 1976.
G. W. Morrison

167 *(below)* Old and new mingle in this panoramic view of Bradford taken near Hammerton Street depot with 55 007 *Pinza* heading the 11.55 to Kings Cross. 13 October 1976.
J. S. Whiteley

168 (*above*) 55 006 *The Fife & Forfar Yeomanry* opens up as it rounds the curve at Chaloners Whin Junction, York, on the Sunday 10.00 Edinburgh-Kings Cross. 24 October 1976.
G. W. Morrison

169 (*below*) 55 006 seen again near Pilmoor, this time travelling at 100 m.p.h., on the 11.30 Edinburgh-Kings Cross. 19 April 1976.
J. S. Whiteley

170 *(above left)* D9000 *Royal Scots Grey* takes the Carlisle line out of Newcastle with the Sunday 10.00 Kings Cross-Edinburgh diverted via Carlisle due to engineering works at Dunbar. 15 November 1970.

I. S. Carr

171 *(below left)* The Newcastle-Carlisle line again sees a Deltic, this time 9009 *Alycidon* on the diverted 08.00 Edinburgh-Kings Cross seen passing Wylam. 24 July 1972.   *I. S. Carr*

172 *(top)* 9003 *Meld* races past Bytham on an up express on 11 September 1971.

P. H. Wells

173 *(middle)* 55 019 *Royal Highland Fusilier* passes beneath a very graceful five-arch bridge near Abbots Ripton on the 10.40 Edinburgh-Kings Cross. 16 October 1976.

J. S. Whiteley

174 *(right)* D9015 *Tulyar* passes Essendine on a down express.

P. H. Wells

175 *(above)* 55 022 *Royal Scots Grey* approaches York on the Sunday 10.00 Edinburgh-Kings Cross whilst 55 009 *Alycidon* which left Kings Cross at the same time accelerates northwards round the sharp curve at Clifton. 26 September 1976.
J. S. Whiteley

176 *(below)* . . . and passing with York Yard North on the left-hand side. *J. S. Whiteley*

Chaloners Whin Junction, York
177 *(above)* 55 003 *Meld* joins the Midland Line from
Sheffield on the 14.00 Kings Cross-Aberdeen. *J. M. Rayner*

178 *(below)* 55 022 *Royal Scots Grey* speeds southwards on
the 08.50 Aberdeen-Kings Cross on 20 March 1976.
J. S. Whiteley

179 *(right)* Carrying the short-lived head-board D9006 descends past Copley Hill towards Leeds Central on the down "West Riding". 12 April 1962.　　*G. W. Morrison*

180 *(below)* 55 007 *Pinza* emerges from Ardsley tunnel on the 12.30 Leeds-Kings Cross on 13 October 1976.

　　　　　　G. W. Morrison

181 (*above*) The up "Flying Scotsman" passing non stop through York headed by 55 016 *Gordon Highlander*. 20 November 1976.   *G. W. Morrison*

182, 183 An extremely rare visitor to York on 20 November 1976 in the shape of class 52 No. 1023 *Western Fusilier* which had worked a special from Kings Cross and is commanding most of the attention in York Shed yard as (*right*) 55 007 *Pinza* passes southbound on a running-in turn on empty stock. *N. Stead Below* 55 001 *St. Paddy* heads northwards on the 11.00 Kings Cross-Edinburgh. It was not to be long before HSTs relegated the Deltics to working enthusiast specials before their final withdrawal in January 1982.

G. W. Morrison

Appendix I

Deltics under construction

184 *(left)* Three-quarter view of power bogie with superstructure erection in background.

185 *(below left)* Overhead view of power bogie.

186 *(below right)* View of superstructure under erection alongside inverted frame and pipe-work.

All photographs GEC Traction Ltd.

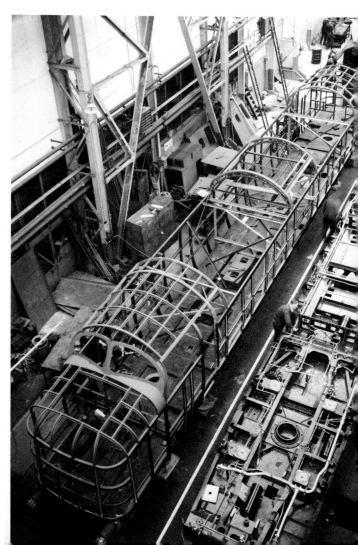

187 *(right)* D9005 being wheeled.

188 *(below left)* Overhead view with one engine room hatch cover removed.

189 *(below right)* Installing one of the power units.

All photographs GEC Traction Ltd.

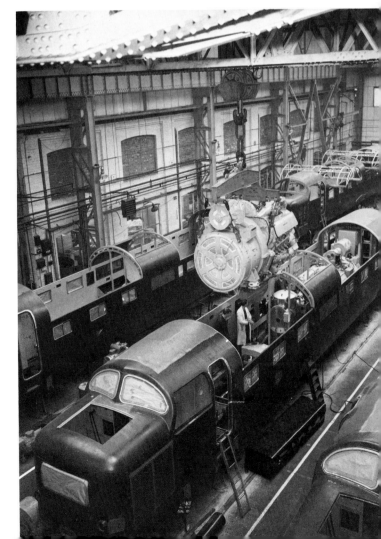

DELTIC CAB INTERIOR —
KEY TO MAIN FEATURES

1. Red light shows bright when No. 1 engine stops.
2. Red light shows bright when No. 2 engine stops.
3. Amber light shows bright if wheel slips.
4. Blue light shows bright when a fault occurs.
5. Automatic Warning Signal cancellation button.
6. A.W.S. "Sunflower" which indicates aspect of the last signal.
7. De-mister switch.
8. Cab heater switch.
9. Cab heater switch.
10. No. 2 Engine start button.
11. No. 1 Engine start button.
12. Earth fault reset button.
13. No. 2 Engine stop button.
14. No. 1 Engine stop button.

15. Master controller.
16. Master switch.
17. Driver's ammeter.
18. Speedometer.
19. Main reservoir air pressure.
20. Train pipe and vacuum gauges.
21. Locomotive brake cylinder pressure.
22. Vacuum/air brake valve.
23. Driver's air brake valve.
24. Windscreen washer.
25. Horn.
26. Driver's safety device.
27. Windscreen wiper control.
28. Windscreen wiper motor.

BRITISH RAIL '55' CLASS d.e. LOCOMOTIVES

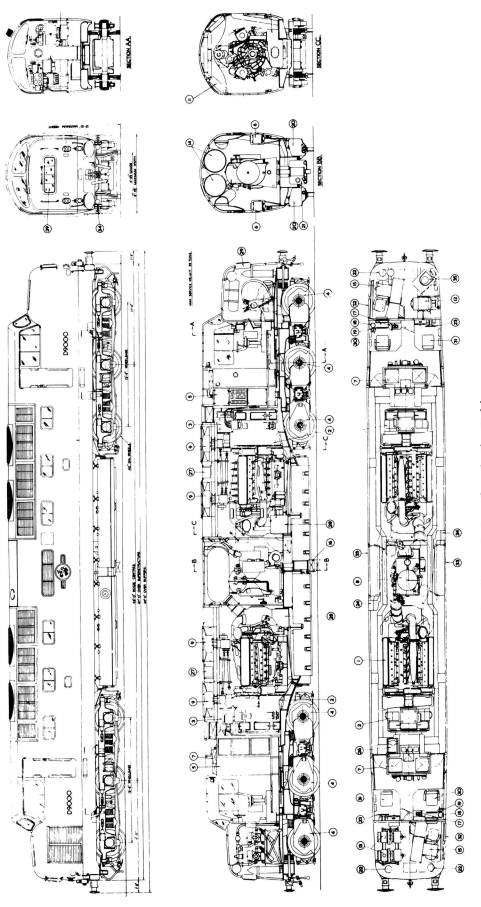

Leading particulars of production Deltics

Engines Two 18-cylinder Napier "Deltic" of 1,650 b.h.p. giving a total b.h.p. of 3,300.
Maximum tractive effort 50.000 lb.
Weight 99 tons.

Axle load 16.5 tons.
Fuel capacity 900 gallons
Driving wheel diameter 3 ft. 7 in.
Maximum speed 100 m.p.h.

Appendix II

Original Number	Date Delivered	Allocation	Name	Date Re-Numbered	New Number	Notes on Names
9000	28.2.61	Haymarket	Royal Scots Grey	w/e 10.4.74	55 022	Name previously carried by LMS "Royal Scot" Class locomotive.
9001	23.2.61	Finsbury Park	St. Paddy	w/e 23.2.74	55 001	Racehorse, won Derby & St. Leger in 1960.
9002	9.3.61	Gateshead	The King's Own Yorkshire Light Infantry	w/e 8.12.73	55 002	Name previously carried by former LNER V2 locomotive.
9003	27.3.61	Finsbury Park	Meld	w/e 23.2.74	55 003	Racehorse, won 1,000 Guineas, The Oaks & St. Leger in 1955.
9004	18.5.61	Haymarket	Queen's Own Highlander	w/e 1.5.74	55 004	Regimental names not previously used on locomotives.
9005	25.5.61	Gateshead	The Prince of Wales's Own Regiment of Yorkshire	w/e 2.2.74	55 005	
9006	29.6.61	Haymarket	The Fife & Forfar Yeomanry	w/e 27.3.74	55 006	
9007	22.6.61	Finsbury Park	Pinza	w/e 16.2.74	55 007	Racehorse, won Derby & King George VI and Queen Elizabeth Stakes 1953.
9008	7.7.61	Gateshead	The Green Howards	w/e 9.2.74	55 008	Different version of name "The Green Howard" previously carried by V2 Class locomotive.
9009	21.7.61	Finsbury Park	Alycidon	w/e 26.1.74	55 009	Racehorse, won Ascot Gold Cup & Goodwood Cup in 1949.
9010	24.7.61	Haymarket	The King's Own Scottish Borderer	w/e 16.6.74	55 010	Different version. "Scottish Borderer" used on "Royal Scot" Class locomotive.
9011	24.8.61	Gateshead	The Royal Northumberland Fusiliers	w/e 16.2.74	55 011	Regimental name not previously used on a locomotive.
9012	4.9.61	Finsbury Park	Crepello	w/e 2.2.74	55 012	Racehorse, won 2000 Guineas & Derby 1957.
9013	14.9.61	Haymarket	The Black Watch	w/e 28.2.74	55 013	Name previously carried by LMS "Royal Scot" Class locomotive.
9014	29.9.61	Gateshead	The Duke of Wellington's Regiment	w/e 2.2.74	55 014	Regimental name not previously used on a locomotive.
9015	13.10.61	Finsbury Park	Tulyar	w/e 2.2.74	55 015	Racehorse, won Derby, St. Leger & Eclipse Stakes in 1952.
9016	27.10.61	Haymarket	Gordon Highlander	w/e 16.3.74	55 016	Name previously used on LNER D.40 and LMS "Royal Scot" Class locomotive.
9017	5.11.61	Gateshead	The Durham Light Infantry	w/e 9.2.74	55 017	Name previously used on former LNER V2 Class locomotive.
9018	24.11.61	Finsbury Park	Ballymoss	w/e 9.2.74	55 018	Racehorse, won St. Leger & King George VI & Queen Elizabeth Stakes 1958.
9019	29.12.61	Haymarket	Royal Highland Fusilier	w/e 22.11.73	55 019	Regimental name not previously used.
9020	12.2.62	Finsbury Park	Nimbus	w/e 10.11.73	55 020	Racehorse, won Derby & 2000 Guineas in 1949.
9021	2.5.62	Haymarket	Argyll & Sutherland Highlander	w/e 2.1.74	55 021	Name previously carried by "Royal Scot" Class locomotive.